How to Open a Bar

An Entrepreneur's
Essential Guide
to Opening, Operating,
and Owning a Bar
or Nightclub

by Simon Pasco

Table of Contents

Introduction

If you are looking to start a bar or nightclub, you've probably already heard countless times that **it is a risky venture**. You are not only competing with other bars — you are competing with every form of nightlife out there! Movies, arcades, strip clubs, or wherever else people find themselves going on a Friday or Saturday night.

Once you have accepted that fact and are sure that you have the resources and back-up plan to take such a risk, your journey to success is still far from over. Starting a bar is a time-intensive and labor-intensive process that demands your utmost attention. It requires you to make intelligent decisions about everything — from the name of your bar, to the price of your drinks, to the trust you establish with your staff. In a word, it is "difficult."

And now that I'm done officially "warning" you, to be perfectly honest, it sounds more difficult than it actually is — as long as you're willing to do your homework. If this is a dream that you truly want to pursue, and one that you think you're capable of excelling at, then you should definitely give it a shot. For the right entrepreneur, opening a bar can be extremely lucrative, and thereby extremely rewarding.

The safest, smartest way to get started is to hatch up a business plan on paper before making any moves. You should have an idea about all the costs — and potential returns — before making a single purchase. And for that, this book will be your handy guide. Here we will discuss how to start with a vision and tweak it to fit your potential market. After that you will learn how to match this revised vision with the practical considerations of owning and operating a successful joint. With diligence and careful planning, you could soon be the owner of the hottest bar in town. Let's get started!

Chapter 1: Building Your Vision

First things first: if you are opening a bar or nightclub, you have to know what you want. Everything from the décor to the music to the menu has to come together through a unified theme, so it is important to have a cohesive vision for the space. You will have a chance to revise this to fit your market, as we discuss in the next chapter, but for now use this as your chance to sketch out all the dreams you have for this baby.

Note that since starting a bar is risky business, those who get involved inevitably invest a piece of themselves in the venture. Often, they put some of their financial assets on the line. Making a risky investment demands foresight into how to make it a successful investment — and knowing what makes you the right person for the job. What can you specifically bring to the table — which of your own skills, background, or tastes will be useful in making your vision a reality? This point, in particular, requires you to look past the foggy haze of the dreams of owning a bar or nightclub and be brutally honest with yourself about your business-sense, so to speak.

If you feel that you don't exactly have the sharpest-honed business sense around, you may want to consider letting a friend or sibling who's more adept at such matters become a part of your project. Keep in mind though that dealing with strangers or acquaintances as business partners is messy because of trust issues, and dealing with friends or family in business can also get messy because personal matters often spill-over into business life — so there's no easy right or wrong road in this scenario.

Your choice should come down to two things — who would I be able to carry out a business relationship with most efficiently, and who would be the best fit in terms of skills for the job that I have in mind — in that order. While great skills can be honed to excellence through experience, someone that you always seem to have friction with in the simplest of matters will never necessarily change in that regard.

Also if you really want to do this, and do it right, you need a vision. You must already have some ideas about what is missing from your neighborhood's nightlife. Are there too many dive bars and no cocktail bars? Is there not a single decent nightclub? When you imagine opening a bar, what exactly do you think of?

Spend a few days to make a list, in your mind or on paper, about *all* the elements you imagine. If you are not sure, ask yourself why exactly you want to do this. Is it because there is great potential for a certain type of bar in the local neighborhood? Do you frequent bars and love the thought of yourself on the other side of the counter? If you're wondering, the first question shows a lot more business acumen and commercial feasibility than the second one. But, the latter doesn't mean that you're not suited to owning such a business — just that you should stay alert, and not get swept into impulsive bad decisions because of the hasty urge to accomplish this dream.

Here are a few ideas to get you thinking:

A sports bar in a large open space and a few giant TV screens that are great for regular large, sports-centered gatherings. Sports paraphernalia hanging on the wall, with great beer brews and excellent carbo-loaded chow like fries and wings.

A speakeasy from another era. A cozy center stage, maybe with a piano, for a cooing vocalist. Small round tables and matching chairs that evoke the French style. One wall lined with bookshelves with great literature from around the world, available for borrowing in a give-one, take-one style. Walls with old postcards, and maybe a photo booth.

A specialty bar that focuses on one type of drink like gin or rum. You have to amass a sizable collection of rare and exclusive alcohols of one type to fill the shelves of such a bar, but it can pay great rewards to be serving cultured regulars exactly what they are looking for. One great option for a specialty bar is a wine bar. With a knowledgeable sommelier on board, a rustic bar with long wooden tables and large crystal glasses can be the perfect setting for eager customers to learn about the ins-and-outs of making and drinking wine. Couple it with a plate of fine cheeses and this becomes the perfect rendezvous point for an intimate gathering.

Consider the following elements, which will both determine your cost structure and shape your vision:

Location

Which neighborhood do you see yourself establishing your bar in? Make sure the locality is a reasonable pick for the ambience you want to establish. Putting a specialty bar in a lower-income neighborhood can be risky, but if the area is gentrifying you can reap great rewards by establishing early. Think about what other bars are in the area. It works well to be closer to people's places of work rather than where they live, as being near places of work often means you are in more urban environments and closer to other similar forms of entertainment. Brainstorming a good locale involves a balance between being central yet being able to set yourself apart.

Once you have a general idea about the type of location where you'd like to set up your business, keep an eye on rising or falling real estate prices in the region. Would you prefer renting your space, or buying one outright? Both approaches have pros and cons, and decisions between the two largely depend on your level of certainty in the feasibility of your business plan.

While both steps require you to check if you can acquire liquor and commercial licenses, the latter would require far deeper investments on your part than the former. However, keep in mind that if you rent a space and your business takes off, you may not always get the option to buy out the space you're currently renting, and other viable commercial spaces may not be available for sale anywhere close by. Also, you should understand that if you run a successful bar or nightclub on a rented space, you give significant leverage to the owner of the space in terms of buy-out lump-sums further in the future. If you already have an area in mind, and wish to purchase a location instead of renting one — you can always keep an eye out for bank-foreclosed commercial spaces which would then be auctioned off for relatively cheaper rates than they would otherwise have cost you. Remember that successful businesses capitalize on opportunities. As saddening as such circumstances may be, their availability may reduce your initial capital investment by significant amounts of money.

Theme

When someone needs to describe your bar, how will they describe it? This is an excellent way to come up with your 15-second elevator pitch — thinking about how you want the bar to be described, what makes it unique from everything else out there, and then taking the concrete steps and investments to get there. A concept unifies the elements of your vision, anchoring the parts in a cohesive whole: an Irish bar with great outdoor seating; a rooftop bar with tiki torches and cushioned lounge areas; a standard dive bar with pool tables and mirrored walls. Think unique, and in the next steps you can tailor this vision to the market and your budget.

Keep in mind that you'll always keep adding elements to your theme so you don't necessarily need to have every inch of the space mapped out right from the start—but it would help you calculate the amount you can accomplish within your allocated budget without the need for outside investors. However, the one thing that you *do* need from the start is your ***hook*** — the one element that sets you apart from other bars around, and which would help you attract new clientele while establishing a regular one (and no, fusion cuisine isn't the answer).

Size

This one is so straightforward that you might have not considered it as a factor. What is the size of the bar? Big, small, long, multi-level? As I'm sure any house owner already knows, the size and layout of spaces have massive effects on the general tone of the place. The size of the bar should ideally fit the theme — sports bars should have ample space for large groups to gather around, a wine bar would be more intimate. The size of the bar will also determine the type of furniture within, and the location of the bar, drinks, and the kitchen relative to the rest of the tables.

If you consider size, you should also consider flow. Essentially, this means that the layout of the location would be such that people shouldn't be inconvenienced by one another. For example, if there's a dais or stage at your location for live bands or singers, the bathrooms shouldn't be located right next to the stage — some people may find it distasteful to have to enter the limelight of the stage every time they want to visit the loo. If you're preparing smaller cubbyholes or booths for more quiet and intimate settings, they should be kept away from acoustic 'sweet-spots' where you may intend to put speakers. If you have a multi-level location, it may work for any kind of bar or club that you may have in mind — but you should be able to build washrooms on multiple levels as well so that people don't always have to keep climbing and descending stairs over and over again. In such a case, consider making space for bars on different levels if you're operating establishments where patrons would get their drinks themselves, rather than be served. Think about what might make a typical night more convenient for your patrons, I'm sure you get the point. Plan ahead, and scout locations accordingly.

Chapter 2: Knowing What Your Market Craves

The laws of supply and demand govern the profit margin of every business, including your entrepreneurial venture. If your vision is what you want to supply, you need to next get to know the market and who your potential customers are and what they will demand. This is the first key step to making your bar successful.

In the last chapter, we asked the question "Is there a single decent nightclub around?" Here we revise that question slightly. It is time to ask, "Are there no decent nightclubs because no one has taken that golden opportunity to open one, or because not enough people around here care to dance?" Understanding your market is the art of matching what you can provide to what people want or need. And remember, people do not always know what they want.

If you are thinking of starting a bar, you are likely to have frequented a fair share of them yourself. Think about your local bars or the place where you would want to start the bar (Important: hopefully these two are the same, because you have to know the area where you want to start the bar, and know it intimately). What is the drinking culture? Are there certain nights when people go out? Do people go out with friends, coworkers, in large groups or small? Are sports integral to the drinking culture? Are there enough trivia nights around, and is there space for more?

This part of your plan won't get completed in days and, in fact, might take weeks. Chances are that if you've struck upon a good location for a bar or nightclub, and there aren't many others around that could satisfy the needs of locals, you won't find any market research data on such areas either. At this stage, it may also be better to keep your ideas largely to yourself unless you want to tip off other prospective nightclub chains to the excellent opportunities provided by the areas you're considering. Instead, enter nightclubs and try to befriend circles of regular clientele. Attempt to establish acquaintanceship *outside* the bar or club, and then try and gain insider perspectives into their likes and dislikes, as well as sources of dissatisfaction, in their usual haunts. While participating in a bar's culture tells you a lot about its pros and cons, you may get better feedback if you're directly communicating with your target clientele as an *insider*. However, maintain casual approaches to this step throughout — some bar owners may not be very friendly if they hear of some random person infiltrating their "dive" and asking very business-oriented questions.

The best way to get ideas is to tap into the larger bar culture. Watch the documentary "Hey Bartender!" about the renewed interest in urban cocktail bars. There are a plethora of books and websites about how to find the perfect property, how to obtain a liquor license, and the new mixology culture reviving cocktails. Read up. Meet with local business owners and owners of entertainment venues in the area. Kindly ask them for advice, remembering that you are requesting a favor in benefiting from their hard-earned business savvy. Some of these people might be future competition, so tread carefully. You may also like to frequent such places a couple of times and get to know the owners a little better, rather than letting them know right off the bat that you intend to be their competition. Approach them as an appreciative customer rather than a possible business rival.

However, this approach may be unethical or seem a little underhanded, and may even give rise to apprehension in you. I can fully understand and appreciate your reluctance to apply it. In such a case, identify a *similar* neighborhood which is on the other end of your city or town from the area within which you wish to operate your bar or club. Approach owners *there* as an appreciative customer and try and understand the logistics of running such establishments over several visits. There are a lot of resources out there and it is your responsibility to fully engage with all of them. Heck, spend some time with Cheers! As an entrepreneur you have to remember that you never know where your next big idea will come from, so it is important to keep your eyes and your ears open.

Always remember that, while you're free to offer talented bartenders and other such personnel better deals than they may currently be receiving, do not poach personnel from the bars or establishments where you have also approached the owners to understand their business better. Usually, such actions escalate into personal rivalries rather than professional competition, which is bad for business.

Chapter 3: Opening the Bar

Opening the bar is about finding the right space at an affordable rent, tweaking it as per your vision, and getting out the word. In a word, it is about **establishment.**

Your Bar's Name

It's the number one advertisement tool you have, so choose wisely. Take some real time to think about this because you are stuck with it once you have decided. The best bars usually have catchy names in order to enhance brand recall.

The name of your bar also reflects upon its personality — however you may have designed its persona. And yes, bars are entities of their own. Just like restaurants and other venues of entertainment, their name is interwoven into their identity. So, if you have a casual bar that you've designed for fun and light entertainment, a serious or very high-brow name would clash and reduce the overall impact on your clientele. After all, if you enter a place named Caesar's Abode and find a Tex-Mex fusion restaurant, wouldn't that leave a negative impression in your mind?

Pay close attention to your vision, and choose an appropriate name. Moreover, one thing that you may want to avoid would be to somehow place your name within the bar's — it would change the focus of the bar from its own merits, and thus place you in the cross-hairs of your patrons' evaluation of the place as well (that's a situation you want to avoid at all costs).

In the end, place yourself in the shoes of your clientele, think about the aspects of the bar or club which you'd appreciate the most, integrate those into the name, and find a witty, short, and catchy way to put it across. This isn't an easy step to take — since you can't change the name of your place once you've publicized it. Studies have shown that, even if the inside of such establishments don't change, repeated alterations in the names causes a store or enterprise to lose the ability to attract new clientele (who view the owners as weak and indecisive), and even cause defections among many regular customers except the fanatically loyal ones. Many people go through as many as hundred and fifty to two hundred names before finalizing a name and logo which would solidify and enhance their brand value. Remember to check all prospective names and logos to ensure that they're not already taken, preferably in the country rather than just the city or state. This would help you further your brand through trademarks and exclusive websites. Also, if your business succeeds and you ever wish to expand into a chain, unique names and logos will allow you to avoid legal hassles further down the line. A good motto for any business is — plan as if you're going to succeed, but remain realistic and be not delusional.

Marketing

Word of mouth is the strongest form of advertising, and this is especially true for bars and nightclubs. Each group of clientele who leaves with far better experiences than they'd *hoped* to achieve, or at least as good, will become the primary chain of marketing which will get you more customers. This means that customers need to feel welcome and safe, as well as appreciated, in your establishment. Remember that the effectiveness of word-of-mouth depends largely on the tone of your bar — since you can't satisfy everyone's needs. At best you will appeal to specific niche demographics within a population overall. Therefore, apart from your tone and ambience, you need to pay specific attention to your target market. For example, if you intend to open your bar in a neighborhood that seems to have loads of gyms and other health-related activity centers, it's reasonable to assume that the neighborhood probably houses a large section of health-conscious people. Therefore, you could create a list of "healthy" cocktails (apart from the alcohol of course), by which I mean calorie-conscious yummy alcoholic drinks, or tasty drinks melded with green veggie smoothies, etc. This would ensure that you'd be satisfying a need that doesn't have any chain of supply anywhere else — or you may also be creating a need (health-conscious cocktails) that people didn't even know they had, but now want sated once you've started serving them.

However, word of mouth alone is a highly unreliable method of marketing in a sound business model — and it takes some time to reciprocate enough returns in forms of new clientele, and thus may slow down the growth of your business in the beginning (in the absence of any other marketing strategy).

Some popular marketing strategies for launching new bars and nightclubs are:

Happy Hours: Provide specific drinks at far cheaper rates during pre-determined hours on particular days. For example: Some new bars offer happy hours from 4 pm to 8 pm every day or on alternate weekdays (not on week-ends). If you've done your research of the competition, you could provide drinks at cheaper rates than their discounted offers during happy hours. While this may reduce your profit margin, this particular strategy works wonders if you want to establish a steady stream of clientele during the slower hours of the week. If your ambience and *hook* are good enough, it may also incite many patrons to return during regular hours with their acquaintances.

Special Nights: By this I mean events like Ladies' nights and all-you-can-drink nights (the latter having set entry charges which would allow patrons to enjoy all the alcohol they can drink, from set menus for such events).

Promotional Partnerships: You could scout businesses in the area which would be interested in hooking up with bars or nightclubs, and set up promotional partnerships which would drive more clientele to both partners. For example: If there's a new restaurant in the area which seems to have great food and already hosts a small regular clientele, but which is looking to expand its operation to host larger crowds — you could create a partnership where clientele to either establishment (yours or theirs) would get discount vouchers which could be redeemed in the other's business. If you partnered up with a great steak place for example, and a client spends more than $140 at their establishment, they could get a single voucher offering a 19% discount on their entire bill at your bar regardless of their order. Or if a client spent more than $250 at your bar, they could be provided with a single voucher offering a 20% discount on their bill at the steakhouse.

Chapter 4: Operating the Bar

Operating the Bar is about Effective Management

You need to have staff you can trust with whom you can establish a system of effectively running the bar. If you can do that, you can set the basis for a well-run, reliable service that keeps your regulars coming back. As you are starting up the bar, it may seem that everything will fall into place once the place is open, but that is far from true. The first few weeks, months, and perhaps years, are essential to establishing a welcoming and consistent culture so people know what to expect. Benefactors will keep coming back to your place when they know what to expect, so put together a systematic flow for how your operations will run before you even open shop.

Know Your Staff

You want to have people you trust behind the bar. The bar counter can be such a fun and socially engaging place that it is easy for bartenders to get carried away. You need to make sure that they remain diligent and do their job, without micromanaging. See if you can get familiar faces behind the bar. Look to your friends to see who has a bartending license, and enlist their help if you know you will have a good working relationship. If there is a local face that everyone recognizes, humbly ask him or her to join the team. Every little bit counts. By building a sense of camaraderie, trust, and timeliness early on, you will be able to battle the first wave of hurdles that hit you as you open for business.

Establish a Culture of Timeliness and Effectiveness

Even if bars and nightclubs operate as suppliers of "Fun", they're still serious businesses nonetheless. Therefore you need to ensure that you have regular schedules for yourself and your employees. Set the opening and closing times of your bar. If your opening times vary, you may lose potential business early in the day since customers who wouldn't trust you to be open would simply take their business elsewhere. Also, while some businesses like pushing their closing times to accommodate customers, that's a sure-shot way of landing in trouble with the law.

Instill Discipline in Yourself and Your Crew

By this I mean: do not drink on the job. While it can be the perfect end to a tiring day, running a club or bar requires being able to stay focused with juggling all the different elements of a business at hand. There are very few ways that lead to mismanagement as surely as operating your business through the haze of intoxication.

Cherish Your Regulars

They are your real assets. With so many options out there for customers, it is a real treasure when you begin to develop a group of customers who visit your establishment regularly. It is important to treat them well, because they already think highly of the bar and are likely to bring their friends or suggest the bar to their acquaintances, if the opportunity arises. Encourage the bartenders to remember their orders, become friendly with them without being invasive, and give them a free drink if they are feeling down. Prove to them that they have made the right choice by coming back to you. The flip side to this point is to remember that high volume — having lots of people coming through the bar, and the tables full —

does not necessarily mean that you have a strong customer base.

Remain Firm When Things Get Unruly

It may happen from time to time, since you're in the business of booze, that things get out of hand. This is why most clubs employ professional bouncers — not violent amateurs, but level-headed professionals who understand the difference between searching for excuses to throw people out, and calmly assessing and stepping in to defuse a potentially violent situation. Even if the miscreants are cherished regulars, you need to establish firm boundaries for appropriate behavior in your *place of business* and either turn them over to the cops, or ban them from entering your premises. While such decisions may be difficult if your business has seen some recent slumps, they're vital for long-term growth through other clientele.

Chapter 5: Owning the Bar

Owning the bar is about keeping it in the black and to make more money than you spend. Owning a bar is a dream for many people, but it takes financial stamina, careful management and planning to cover your ground.

The Costs

Liquor Licensing: Owning a liquor license is expensive, and often one of the most cost-prohibitive things about owning a bar. It involves several legal requirements that need to be followed and fulfilled at all times. Any lax in alertness while you run your business may well cost you this piece of paper — which would unfortunately also mean that you can no longer feasibly operate a *bar.*

The Property: Rent will include a security deposit and the first few months of rent, depending on the landlord. In addition to rent, property requires upkeep such as painting, plumbing, changes to flooring if necessary, etc. Commercial spaces may also require specific licenses depending on your city, which may also add to the costs. In addition, some states require specific land taxes to be paid for certain kinds of establishments, so it becomes important to figure out all the property-related legal costs along with other payables during the research phase.

Supplies: Stocking inventory can be a tricky mathematical exercise. This depends on many factors which you need to consider while deciding on sizes of future orders. The objective is to always have enough supplies on stock to last you a specific period, say five days or a week, without having too much excess that would lie around unsold on the shelves. You will also constantly keep tweaking your inventory orders from your distribution chain, as and when you see a change in the dominant tastes of your clientele. This exercise doesn't just apply to your liquor stocks, but produce and ingredients for foods served at your establishment as well. Your first menu — food or alcohol — will by no means remain the exact same menu which you'll be providing years down the line.

Operational Safety: Apart from the costs mentioned above, remember that many bars and nightclubs deal with large amounts of cash each day, which needs to be counted and safely stored away. Unless you plan to drive to your bank and deposit sums of cash each morning, you may want to invest in a sturdy safe in your office, which you can then empty — with your bouncer or a bodyguard, if necessary — and deposit in your bank at regular intervals. Of course, you could also look at the feasibility of operating as a card-only business if you think that would work out for the better.

Payroll: You need to also account for payroll in your costs. This would include your own paycheck, bartenders, maintenance staff, servers, chefs for the kitchen, any specialty liquor stewards (like sommeliers), payment counter staff if any, bouncers, guards, etc. Since great bartenders are sometimes hard to find, they may require a larger paycheck than most others on your staff — but if you want to avoid hemorrhaging money through your payroll costs, it's best to hire selective but skilled staff members rather than take on an ill-trained crowd who turns out to be more expensive to deal with in the long term.

You may also incur extra costs during the course of your operation, from printing for promotional material, to paying local stations or celebrities to talk about your venue if possible, to hiring cabs to take away clientele if they're too drunk to drive (keep their car keys for their safety, and ask them to reimburse you for cab fares when they return for their car, if you wish — customers with integrity wouldn't mind, and you would develop a reputation for watching out for the safety of your customers, etc.) However, apart from these gross costs listed above, you should identify every possible unique cost which applies to you depending on your theme and location, and account for them in your business plan if you want to get the most accurate picture before you take the first step.

Conclusion

Opening a bar is hard work. It takes long nights, diligence, and attention to detail. It requires multi-tasking and having a sharp focus on a vision you want to achieve. But, to be perfectly honest, it sounds more difficult than it actually is — as long as you do your homework properly. Just like every other business, operating bars and nightclubs is about supply and demand — the building blocks of every market. However, owing to the "razzle-dazzle" of this particular business, it's awfully tempting to either circumnavigate the law to obtain more profit, or to get lost in its glamor and make poorly thought out decisions based on hasty urges to get closer to achieving success — which is where most people in this business fail. It has less to do with their original plan being faulty, and more to do with them having lost track since they stopped making sound business decisions.

A simple trick to finding out whether you did enough background homework is this: when you've done bare-minimal shallow research, the logistics of the business will seem confusing and quite difficult to penetrate which — though you may still be optimistic — may result in your final plan being based more on hope and fiction rather than facts, and you'll know it. If you've dug deeper into the bar business, and are being pulled in different directions which is causing you to despair over your dreams of opening a bar or club, the problem wouldn't be that you haven't done your homework. It is more likely that you're being indecisive and need to settle on the theme and elements based on what your customers need the most and which would appeal to your sensibilities as well. Lastly, if you've done your research, have decided on the demands which you'll meet through your business, and have accounted for every single cost that you can think of — your plan will be doable with *decent* (not heavy) returns, which is where a good business usually falls if the owner is being realistic rather than optimistic.

If your assessment of the customers, location, and theme were spot on, you'll find yourself drawing in more money than you originally calculated within three months of your establishment's opening. That's primarily because it's somewhat easier to account for possible costs and problems and prepare for it, than it is to account for unexpected good luck and windfalls. But as they say, good luck only comes to those who prepare for the worst.

In the end, while you may lose sleep at first, remember to be open to tweaking your plans as needed and things will be fine! Most importantly, remember to have fun — because someone who's miserable at their job will hit their limits at mediocrity. You'll need to stay upbeat, look for silver linings, and develop a positive attitude if you wish to become successful in this particular business without letting it affect you or your family life.

Finally, I'd like to thank you for purchasing this book! If you enjoyed it or found it helpful, I'd greatly appreciate it if you'd take a moment to leave a review on Amazon. Thank you!